How to Become a Real Estate Investor

**A Practical Guide on
How to
Build Wealth
with
Real Estate**

Table of Contents

Introduction

Are you thinking about becoming a real estate investor? There are some points that you should consider before you begin to invest in real estate that could decide if you succeed or fail.

The first thing you should consider when investing in real estate is can you afford it? Real estate investing is an expensive thing to begin to do and you need to take a look at your budget.

You will probably have to make a real estate investment loan so you can invest in your real estate but can you pay that loan back? To invest in real estate is a big commitment and you are going to have to know if you are going to be able to afford it before you begin.

You need to decide why you are investing in real estate. If you are investing for your family you should check out the papers and formalities of the land such as water, road connectivity to the estate and electricity, and also how near to schools, shops, etc. the estate is located.

If the house is a home you are investing in you should take a walk through the interior to make sure there are no faults or repairs needed.

If you are buying the estate solely for the purpose of reselling it in the future it is very important that you do a lot of research on the estate. You need to find out how much of an appreciation the land goes through and also calculate which areas are going to bring you the best profit.

This is important because you do not want to go out and buy an estate on land that is not in demand.

The next point to consider before investing in real estate is to choose a good real estate agent. When choosing a real estate agent you should choose one who has a good market knowledge and one who knows the latest trend of the real estate market.

You also need to choose an agent who is reliable as the bargain of the real estate investment lies solely on the agent's knowledge and trust. If you choose a bad real estate agent you could end up with a bad bargain and many problems so choose wisely.

After reading this book you should walk out knowing how to begin to invest in real estate and be on your way to success.

Chapter 1

What is Real Estate Investment?

The question, "What is real estate investing?" cannot be answered without considering first its textbook definition and then its conceptual definition.

The Academic Definition

Real estate has been defined as land (or immovable property) along with anything permanently affixed to the land such as buildings, and investment is the act of using money to purchase property for the sole purpose of holding or leasing for income.

It is safe to say then (combining both definitions) that real estate investing involves the acquisition of real estate (or investment in real estate) for purposes of generating income, making a profit, and acquiring wealth.

The Conceptual Definition

Leverage. In contrast to stock investments (which usually require more equity from the investor), it is possible to leverage a real estate investment (heavily).

With a real estate investment, you can use other people's money to magnify your rate of return and control a much larger investment otherwise not possible.

Tax Shelter. Real estate investing provides tax benefits. There are yields on annual after-tax cash flows, equity buildup through appreciation of the asset, and cash flow after tax upon sale.

Non-Monetary Returns. Real estate investment provides pride of ownership, the security that you control ownership, and portfolio diversification.

Real estate investing is not a bed of roses, though. Real estate investment does require capital, there are risks, and rental property can be management-intensive. On the other hand, the car you drive required capital, it involves risk driving, and it certainly requires management.

The difference is that a car is not a source of wealth. Develop a real estate investment goal. What do you want to achieve, and by when do you want to achieve it? What rate of return do you expect to want to receive on moneys you pull out of your home or bank account to purchase an investment property given the risk?

Learn what returns you should look for, and how to compute them. You cannot succeed in music unless you can read music. Invest in a good real estate investing course or real estate investment software where you can learn how to run the returns and compute the formulas.

Be wary of 'get rich' schemes. There are many so-called gurus ready to teach you how to make millions with real estate investment property. But let logic be your guide; we believe that nobody who finds a gold mine publishes a map.

Create a relationship with a real estate professional that knows the local real estate market and understands rental property.

It will not advance your investment objectives to spend time with the "agent of the year" unless that person knows about investment property and is adequately prepared to help you correctly procure it. Find an agent that understands real estate investing.

That real estate investing is a business about owning a piece of ground that, when researched and purchased sensibly by impartial numbers and careful management, and with reasonable goals and caution, will likely be more valuable tomorrow than it is today.

Chapter 2

How to Make Money Investing in Real Estate

Few people even consider making money in real estate investing because they think it to be extremely difficult. Most people will also rather go through a realtor company or property broker to help them buy their homes but if they knew that it was possible to save thousands of Dollars by having a little knowledge on how real estate works, they would definitely rather do it on their own.

If you visit any real estate website, there is always a lot of technical terms and jargon written on it making dealing in property matters look seriously complicated. In reality this is not so, and with a little reading and research you can buy your own home and even become involved in real estate investing that can make you a lot of money in both the short and long term if it pleases you.

The Right Way to Invest in Real Estate for Maximum Returns

It does not really matter whether you already own your own home or are a new home buyer. Certain inside information can help you secure land and homes at a fraction of their value if you know how it is done.

This is through the purchase of tax lien properties and foreclosed homes which can be located all over the United States. Knowing where to find these listings and how to go about buying and selling these homes can make real estate investing hugely lucrative.

It is possible to own a luxury home you would never have considered possible just by doing a little research, and finding out where y to get insider information. Armed with this knowledge making money with real estate investing will become second nature and you can build wealth and own the home of your dreams quite easily.

Invest in Foreclosed Homes and Tax Lien Properties

It is not only professional realtors and property investment brokers that can make money on foreclosed homes and tax lien properties; anyone can do it if they had the right knowledge. Many realtors already have the inside information and have become extremely wealthy knowing how to secure foreclosed homes and tax lien properties which they purchase and sell, at huge profits to home buyers who are none the wiser.

You will find that in the majority of cases realtors live in large luxury homes as well that have been procured from sales of this nature.

Real estate investing for the long term is considered far more sensible than short term property buying and selling because this will allow you to absorb any market fluctuations but either way the value of properties are apt to increase over the longer term.

Real estate investing with knowledge on how to purchase tax lien homes and foreclosed properties allows you to enjoy the best of both worlds. Although location is considered important when looking at real estate investing; buying and selling of tax liens and foreclosure properties can be done anywhere all over the United States and resold for fast returns.

Investing in Real Estate for Maximum Profits

If you are looking for property for sale as an investment then this a very attractive way of making a good return on your money but certain factors need to be taken into consideration to ensure you get maximum returns.

If you do not know much about investing in real estate then once again it is certainly sensible to do your homework first. Sometimes investing in real estate can be more lucrative by doing it yourself rather than using the services of a realtor.

The most important factors that must be considered in property investment are the location and the future potential of the property.

Unless you know the secrets of making fast returns on investment property then investing in real estate is better over long term periods. Maximum return can be gained by buying the land and cheap homes at a low price and waiting for a while for values to increase as they are developed.

There are certain niches in the real estate market that allow fast maximum returns on real estate investing.

People in the know however would prefer keeping this to themselves. A little research can open many doors in the property for sale market and whether you are a new home buyer or seeking investment in real estate it can be incredibly rewarding.

Why Invest in Real Estate?

Those who don't know much about real estate tend to ask the question "Why should I invest in real estate?" When I'm asked that question, I tend to give the very watered-down answer that investing in real estate is a lot less volatile than investing in the stock market.

If the person wants more information, I go into more detail with some of the reasons why real estate investing is not only one of the most lucrative ways to invest, but also one of the safest.

Appreciation - With respect to rental properties, investment properties tend to appreciate (increase) in value. So in layman's terms, the property, over time, is going to be worth more than what you initially paid for it, hence, a TRUE investment, and not an expense disguised as a potential investment.

Rental Income - Going hand-in-hand with appreciation is rental income. This is like the win-win situation. Not only is your property increasing in value, but someone other than yourself is making the payments on YOUR property.

Anything over what you are required to pay for the property is INCOME. So if you are required to pay $800 for the property, and the renter pays $1100 in rent, you receive an income of $300 for that property.

Duplication - staying with the rental theme, when a renter pays down your mortgage (amortization), you begin to accumulate equity in the property. You can, in turn, use this equity to fund more deals, and duplicate the investing process.

Lump Sums of Money - While renting creates a steady stream of income, other real estate investing techniques like "flipping" can create large chunks of money. Some "flipping" techniques include wholesaling, rehabbing, and short sales.

Essentially, in all of these techniques, the investor contracts or buys a property under market value and in a short period of time, resells the property for more then the original contract or purchase price.

To give a rehabbing example, if I purchase a property for $50,000 and it costs me $30,000 to repair/fix up the property, I have invested a total of $80,000. Well, I knew before I bought the property that I could resell the property for $130,000. I have a potential gross profit of $50,000. Not bad!

Little-to-No Out of Pocket Investing - Some real estate investment strategies require little-to-no money "out of pocket." Wholesaling and "subject to" deals are just two examples of ways to invest with little to no money out of pocket, that can yield substantial returns.

So if you ask "why should I invest in real estate?" I will give you the standard answer first, but if you want to know more, you will be given many reasons as to why real estate investing is the safest and most lucrative way to invest.

Benefits of Real Estate

In your everyday life you might have listened or read about the real estate. Real estate is all about the selling and purchasing and even the lending of the lands, houses and properties.

Now there are many people who are often interested in the investment stages of the real estate but they eventually turn off their minds as they are not much aware from the advantages of the real estate.

Real estate is one of such sectors in the world that does not offer and harms and disadvantages and it is all the time filled with the benefits and benefits. In this book I will lead you into the benefits of investing in real eastate.

In the real estate investment the person gets the sole and just chance of increasing the financial level and money making in his or her account. It may also allow the portfolios to get much higher in height as well.

Many people think that investing in the real estate would serve them with tremendous dangers but that's not true anymore because this sector has been so far appeared to be much beneficial as compare to the other investment divisions in whole world.

The person is given the full proof guarantee that he or she will never face any dangers or risk in the real estate investment. No matter that whether the property has been placed on a healthy land or the rough place it will eventually concludes with the higher rates of the land and finally it grants the profit to the person.

In addition, if the person wants to get the loan from the bank then being the real estate investor it even becomes much easier and convenient for the person to purchase the loan much quickly. On the other side he or she may even get higher interest rates as well that is normally known as the profit of the land.

The person is just required to choose down the most appropriate land that would increase the price rate in just one sight. Real estate investment can be undertaken in all the sectors including the commercial, industrial and even agricultural.

If the property has been sold in the higher price than you can further continue to purchase some other fine-looking land at the same rate and can even sell it on the triple amount. In this way it will in the end increases your bank account with money.

On the other side for making more know how about the investment stages the person can take the assistance from the real estate advisor who can carry out the functions much effectively and conveniently.

On the whole we are sure that all such people who have the misconceptions about the real estate they would have gain much information now. So if you are planning for making the investment in the real estate then perform or and we are sure that this business would just serve you with success sand advantages.

Chapter 3

How to Successfully Invest in Real Estate for Beginners

We all are thinking about it and some of us are actually taking action and getting their hands on real estate investment properties. The longer the New York Stock Exchange doesn't produce desirable returns, the more people are starting with real estate investments.

For most of us the obvious choice of properties are single family homes. Although you can invest in real estate without owning a home, most people follow the experience they made while purchasing their own home. This is familiar ground and the learning curve for doing a real estate deal of this type is pretty slim.

Of course there is a drawback with this approach. The competition is fierce and there are markets where investors are artificially driving up the cost of the properties while completely discouraging first time home buyers. If this is the case, the burst of the real estate bubble is just a matter of time.

How do you avoid these situations and still successfully invest in real estate? How do you get ahead of the competition and be prepared for bad times in real estate investments as well? The only answer I have is commercial real estate.

Why commercial real estate you might ask? Commercial real estate is a solid investment in good and bad times of the local real estate market. The commercial real estate I'm referring to are multi unit apartment buildings.

Yes you will become a landlord and No you don't have to do the work by yourself. You are the owner and not the manager of the apartment building. The cost of owning and managing the building is part of your expenses and will be covered by the rent income.

Apartment buildings are considered commercial real estate if there are 5 or more units. To make the numbers work you should consider to either own multiple small apartment buildings or you should opt for bigger buildings.

This will keep the expense to income ratio at a positive cash flow. Owning rental properties is all about positive cash flow.

With investing in single family homes it is easy to achieve positive cash flow. Even if your rent income doesn't cover your expenses 100%, the appreciation of the house will contribute to the positive cash flow. With commercial real estate the rules are different.

While single family homes are appraised by the value of recent sales of similar homes in your neighborhood, commercial real estate doesn't care about the value appreciation of other buildings.

The value of the property is solely based on the rent income. To increase the value of a commercial real estate you need to find a way to increase the rent income. The formula on how this is calculated would be too much for this short article. I listed a few very helpful books where you can find all the details.

What's another advantage to invest in commercial real estate? Commercial real estate financing is completely different than financing a single family home. While financing a single family home you are at the mercy of lenders who want to make sure that you are in the position to pay for the house with your personal income.

Commercial real estate financing is based in the properties ability to produce positive cash flow and to cover the financing cost.

After reading all these information about commercial real estate you want to go out there and dive into the deals. Not so fast. First, you need to learn as much about real estate as possible. In commercial real estate you're dealing with professionals.

If you come across too much as a newbie you will waste these guys's time and your commercial real estate career ended before it actually started. Second, no commercial real estate lender will lend you any money if you can't show at least a little bit of real estate investment experience.

What's the solution to this? Go out there and do one or two single family home deals yourself. It doesn't matter if you make huge profits to start off with. Most newbie investors are losing money on their first deal anyway. If you can manage to show positive cash flow with your single family home deals you are ahead of the pack.

My advice, buy a small single family home in a decent neighborhood and rent it out immediately. This will keep your out of the pocket expenses at a minimum and you will have rent income to cover for your monthly expenses. Bonus, you gain experience as an investor and as a landlord.

Here's another observation I made during my real estate investment career. Most people like to analyze, learn, discuss and analyze some more. They never actually got to do a real estate deal. They love to talk about real estate investments, but never did it themselves.

My approach to real estate investment was simple.

— I bought some books about real estate investment.
— I read every single one of them.
— I put together a simple plan on how I want to get started.
— I started looking for properties.
— I bought my first investment property 30 days after I started reading my first book.
— I made positive cash flow with all of my properties so far.

What is my point? You have to go out there and practice what you've learned. The only valid credential in the real estate business is practical experience.

Having a couple of deals under your belt, you can go out there and start looking at commercial real estate and even impress seasoned investors with your knowledge. Because you made this experience by yourself and you know what you're talking about.

How to Start Investing in Real Estate Guide

Many people are discovering that building home, renovating properties, and selling real estate for profit is a great way to make a living. But unless you know how to start investing in real estate, you're left out in the cold. How can you get involved, and get in on the all cash flow action?

If you want to know how to start investing in real estate, you're on the right track. Real estate investing isn't something you can jump into; there are skills that need to be learned before success can happen.

Learning how to start investing in real estate is important, because if you don't know what you're doing then you don't stand a good chance of making money. And money is what real estate investing in all about.

In fact, you'll need money just to get the start you need. Real estate investors spend their own money to buy property, then spend even more of their money to get that property ready for sale. The goal of all of this is to spend less money than what the property is eventually sold for.

This is how real estate investors make their profit, and how many of them make their living. But money isn't all you need to start investing in real estate.

For those who have the money, time, and smarts to make real estate a success, property investments can pay off in a big way. But real estate investing isn't something that everyone can do.

If you want to know how to start investing in real estate, you have to be committed to the property you buy. It's your money, it's your future, and you'll probably want to take a very hands-on approach to make sure your investment brings back a great profit.

In order to succeed at real estate investing, the property you invest in must be sold. To get your money back, and to get that profit that's so needed, you have to give buyers what they want.

You want the property you're selling to be attractive, livable, and worth all the time and effort you put into it. Budget for renovations carefully, and try to stick within these financial constraints. The more you spend on your property, the smaller your profits will be. But it's a fine line to walk - spend too little, and you may not get the sale price you're asking for.

To get started investing in real estate, pay attention to the property market. Find out what's selling, for how much, and in what areas. Some areas are going to have properties that take a long time to sell, and you may not want to waste your time here.

Choose hot locations, good properties, and something that's in your budget. Running out of money when you're investing in real estate means losing your entire investment. You have to finish what you started, so many sure you don't put all your money into just one property.

When you know how to start investing in real estate, you open up great potential for your future success.

Chapter 4

How to Invest in Real Estate Without Using Your Own Money

Real estate investment has gained popularity over the last five decades. Although this market has numerous opportunities for large profits, owning and purchasing real estate is complex compared to bond and stock investment.

It is thus, crucial to learn how to invest in real estate for one to increase their wealth. The following sections describe various forms of real estate investment and what they entail.

Fundamental Rental Properties

This is the oldest form of investment. In this instance, an investor will purchase property and rent it to tenants. The landlord will then be responsible for mortgage payments, taxes and property costs. Ideally, landlords' charges cover these mentioned costs.

In other cases, the landlord may charge extra to cover costs until mortgage repayment but, it is strategic to exercise patience and only charge for expenses until the payment of the mortgage. At this time, most of the rent will turn into profit.

Moreover, property will have value appreciation during the mortgage course. In this regard, the landlord's asset will be more valuable. There are some downsides to what may appear like a perfect investment.

One can end up with tenants who destroy property or worse, lack tenants in the first place. This leaves one with a negative flow of cash. There is also the issue of locating the correct property.

One should choose an area with low vacancy rates besides an area where individuals will prefer to rent. One should note that this form of investment comes with enormous responsibilities.

Real Estate Investment Factions

These resemble mutual funds for leasing properties. For those who wish to own rental properties but do not want the hassles of being landlords, this provides a good solution for them.

In this case, a company will purchase or construct a set of condos or apartment blocks and permit investors to purchase them through the corporation, thereby, joining the faction. One investor can own multiple or a single unit but the company running the investment faction manages every unit.

In return for management, the company takes a rent percentage. Investment group quality relies wholly on the company providing it. Theoretically, it is safe to invest in real estate, but factions are susceptible to similar charges that irk the mutual fund sector. Again, research plays a vital role in knowing how to invest in real estate.

Trading in Real Estate

These traders represent a different breed from the typical purchase-and rent landlords. They purchase properties with the aim of holding them temporarily, frequently for 3-4 months after which they sell the property for profit.

This method is also termed flipping properties. It occurs on the basis of purchasing properties that are either considerably undervalued or exist in extremely hot markets.

In my earlier book, "A Simple Guide To Investing in Turnaround Stocks" I made mention that "when you see the amount of houses on the market start shrinking, the demand is getting higher and prices will soon be on the rise again".

Furthermore, the sale of homes is a seasonal thing, people tend to buy property more at certain times of the year, so don't compare the numbers from one month to the next, compare them to the same month from a year ago. Your real estate agent can help compile and read these statistics. When the housing stock starts to shrink and the prices start to rise, you'll know we've gone around the corner.

REITs

These are investment trusts that emerge when corporations use investors' money to operate and buy income properties. People trade and purchase them on the main exchanges similar to other stocks.

This form of investment does not include income tax from the corporate whereas, regular companies would incur profit tax during which they would have to allocate profits as dividend should they choose to do so.

Now that you know some of the basic terminology of investing in real estate, you're ready to find out how to do it without you own money.

Chapter 5

Choosing a Real Estate School

Risks are that you may be recognizing getting work within the field of real estate. Assuming that this is the situation, you are likewise undoubtedly intrigued by studying more about real estate school. All things considered, fortunately, you have gone to the correct place.

Here, we will take a much closer get a load of real estate school, and spotting a school around there to furnish you with the real estate courses that you require.You have pondered regardless of whether you really require real estate school.

The most incredibly foremost thing for you to look into is the way that in place for you to end up being a real estate executor in any state, you are determined to be needed to take real estate instructional classes.

This is where the vitality of real estate school goes in. With a specific end goal, which is to take the classes that you are determined to require with a specific end goal, which is to arrange yourself for the real estate authorizing procedure and to meet your state's educating prerequisites, you will revisit real estate school.

With everything taken into account, with a specific end goal, which is to acquire work in real estate, real estate school is something that should be needed of you to go to, paying little heed to in the event that you feel the need to or not.

Spotting a real estate school here is not hard, with the assumption that you have a great thought of what it is that you are searching for. Some of the time you will identify the courses that are wanting to finish your state's necessities for ending up being a real estate operator at your neighborhood group school.

More regularly, be that as it may, you will identify a genuine real estate school here which has these classes to award you. Some real estate offices in fact have their particular real estate school, so as to arrange you for ending up being a real estate operator at their office. A different one of the things that you may be pondering about is what the price of real estate school is.

Actually, this expense will shift consistent with numerous contrasting components. One of the fundamental things that it will rely on is assuming that you are moving toward going to a real estate school or a group university.

The mean cost of real estate school classes is in the middle of several hundred and a couple hundred dollars, while the normal cost of neighborhood school classes is amidst four hundred and five hundred dollars.

While some folks may recognize the price of an exact real estate school engaging, the risks are that you may prefer to choose to revisit a group university, as they regularly may be more reputable.

Obviously, this is absolutely not the case depending on if you know that the real estate school which you have been contemplating revisiting has a particularly reputable name moreover.As you would be able to see, there is much to know with regards to real estate school.

Depending on if this is something that you are contemplating yourself, the risks are that you will doubtlessly prefer to give a ton of thought to the real estate school which you are wanting on deciding on to go to.

Chapter 6

Having Financial Goals When Investing in Real Estate

Savvy investing in real estate requires setting goals. That is because the destination has to be known before the road to get there becomes clear. First, it will force the investor to know their current financial status.

It will also shape decisions about how long to hold onto a property, and will keep the investor from making emotional decisions that leads them to an over-extension of debt. Without those goals, the investors will just wander around making purchases without objective facts to guide them.

Know the Big Picture

One of the best benefits of setting goals for investing in real estate is that it forces the investor to do a complete analysis of their current financial status. There is just no way to know how long it will take you to reach a goal, or how much initially to invest, if the starting point is not known.

This involves tracking income and expenses to determine a net worth. A good CPA, or certified public accountant, can help wade through these numbers.

Short-Term Goals

Start with setting short-term goals. These can be anywhere from a few months to a couple of years. What kind of cash flow will be necessary? Some of the possible goals might include establishing an emergency fund, a vacation fund, or just a fund to increase the standard of living.

Knowing these goals can help decide what kind of investment property will produce the desired outcome. For example, flipping houses is riskier but offers a quicker return.

Long-Term Goals

Most people investing in real estate however, are in it for the long haul; long-term goals are more relevant. Look at expected major expenses such as retirement needs, college expenses, or maybe major vacations.

Match the needs to the goals, and do not make the mistake of over-reaching. Remember- the larger the return, the greater the risk. Failing to keep this in mind can have disastrous results.

Compare Financing Needs versus Goals

After determining the short-term and long-term goals, the next step is to determine if those goals are realistic. Part of this process is reconciling the goals with the financing needs. How much is available to put into the investment property and how much would need to be financed?

If the financing needs are too great, those goals may need to be re-evaluated. Knowing the goals will ensure that only what is necessary is actually borrowed.

Taking the Emotions Out

Investing in real estate can be an emotional decision, but this is dangerous. It leads to buying an investment property based on how much the property is liked, or being caught up in the excitement of the moment.

As a result, an investor might purchase a property that will not produce a return, or it might have serious flaws. Setting goals and basing the decision on objective factors help reduce the emotion factor.

In the end, setting goals will greatly benefit anyone interested in investing in real estate. Both short-term and long-term goals should be considered, as well as a careful analysis of the current financial status.

Basing decisions on objective facts will help ensure a greater, more secure investment. Think of it this way - knowing where to go determines how to get there.

Chapter 7

How to Get Your Exciting Real Estate License and What Does it Offer?

Real Estate is exciting and a very unique career. It has many different careers within real estate itself. You may become a real estate agent, property manager, luxury home specialist and so one, all of which need to have a real estate license.

Let's break down what you need to obtain a real estate license. Please note that these are general requirements for the state of Florida and each state varies.

First to obtain your real estate license you will need to do a 63-hours pre licensing course. Many online educational Real Estate sites offer this and can be done in the comfort of your home. If you are more of an In class person, your local community college might offer the course.

When taken in actual class, the course may take 4 to 6 weeks due to their scheduling. Online classes you can do at your own pace. So if you want, you may do the entire course in one week.

Below are some requirements for the state of Florida to obtain your Real Estate License

General Requirements:

Must be 18 Years of age, have a high school diploma or GED to get your Real Estate License.

Educational Requirements:

Complete the 63-hours pre licensing course and pass.

Exam and Application Requirements:

Submit a completed real estate license application, submit your finger prints and pay any fees associated.

Pass the Florida Real Estate Sales Associate state exam with at least a score of 75 points out of 100 points or pass the Florida Real Estate Law exam with a score of 30 points out of 40 points.

Activate your license with a real estate broker using the DBPR proper forms or can be activated online by your broker.

These are the basic steps needed to obtain your real estate license in Florida. How to get your real estate license sounds easy and to some extent, it is. However, the exam and amount of studying should not be taken lightly.

I would recommend searching online a bit more before you decide on a real estate license. If you want to make a career change, this is definitely a great one.

So How Do You Actually Start in Real Estate and What Does it Offer?

Firstly of course once you have got your real estate license, activate it with a broker. This is where you have to decide what path you want in Real Estate. Different companies offer different options, splits, fees, training and so on. Let's take for example:

Property Management: It is best to search for local property management companies. There are also national property management companies which you can join. Once you join them, thru out your time in this field, you'll gain knowledge and experience on all legal aspects of property management.

There are a lot of them, from how to evict a tenant to how to post the notices on their door and within what time frames. Property management involves a lot of work and at the same time is rewarding.

Many agents lean towards this field due to the steady stream of monthly income. Others don't want to deal with the tenant headaches. Example, if you manage 150 units and average a 10% call rate, that would be 15 different issues to deal with during that month.

These can be from A/C units not working, to plumbing issues; tenants locked out of their homes and need access, to tenants disturbing other neighbors. One the bright side that means 135 units won't cause any issues. On average, the management companies charge around 10% of the monthly rent to owners (All Companies and State are different), in return, you as on agent might get a percentage of that. Since all companies offer different payments, let's just average a monthly income for the company.

Let's say 150 units rented for $1000 each monthly that would be 10% of $1000 which is $100 X 150 units 'equals' $15K monthly income. Now you see the steady income I mentioned above.

Luxury Real Estate: This also a very nice niche in real estate once you obtain your license. There are pros and cons as there is with Property Management. When speaking about luxury real estate we are speaking about homes from 1M and up.

The obvious benefit to this is the amount of money you earn on each transaction. Example, 1M sale at 3% commission gets you 30K income, now reduce your splits with your broker, let says 80/20 split, agent would receive $24k commission, do that 4 times a year and you are at 96K. Not bad at all for going to a pre licensing 63-hours course.

Let's point out the cons. It's not as easy as it sounds or as seen on TV. This market is more of a referral based market. You can definitely do it without referral, but at some point, you need to have those buyers or sellers in your sphere. The cost to reach this price range is very costly upfront.

We are talking about a marketing campaign in the range of 4k to 5k a month minimum in advertising within those areas. After a few months of the campaign you might receive a few calls from sellers or buyers.

There is a lot more to it than just mailing, it needs to be done the proper way. Thus a large investment is needed to start right of the bat in that price range.

Real Estate Agent: The two previous paths don't appear to everyone, I would say 90% of agents go with the traditional real estate agent path. This path in a sense leads to the two previous ones as well.

As you are in the field, you'll be learning from other agents, property managers and so on. Why so many agents go with the traditional real estate agent is due to its training and perhaps quicker income earning. If you put in the work, you can earning income in as little as 30 days, while property management and luxury real estate does take its time for the business to start coming in.

The cons of this path is the amount of training, start up and hard work you will need to put upfront due to inexperience and mistakes you will make before have a steady and stable income (whatever stable means to you).

Agents usually earn 3% of whatever the sale amount of the home is. Example, 200K home, real estate commission would be 6K, let's take the same split as before 80/20, agent receives $4,800 X 1 a month X 12, agent would earn $57,600 yearly.

Not bad at all. Do keep in mind that some, the majority or most real estate companies do charge a transaction fee, desk if, yearly fee and so on.

All in all, the path when you obtain your real estate licenses totally depends on you. Do note that whichever you decide on will require hard work, countless hours of training and possibly working Saturdays and Sundays.

All of these have their pros and cons. There is a lot more to each of these then I described and you should research more shall you want a real estate career.

Chapter 8

Real Estate Loan (Mortgage) - Understanding the Concept

Real estate loan is what a lot of people use to buy their home. Real estate loans have been instrumental in bringing joy to people by making that unaffordable house affordable. Some real estate investors too make use of real estate loans for buying properties.

However, real estate loan is not free money and anyone who buys real estate or plans to buy real estate using real estate loan must understand the concept of real estate loan very clearly.

Real estate loan (also known as mortgage) is the money that you borrow from someone (a financial institution i.e. a mortgage lender) for the purpose of buying a property. The real estate loan generally covers a part of your purchase price and the remaining portion has to be paid by you upfront i.e. as down payment.

The amount (i.e. the percentage of total purchase price) that you have to pay as down payment is dependent on a number of factors and you can generally reduce it to even 5% by going for mortgage insurance.

FHA and VA loans (i.e. mortgage insurances through FHA and VA) reduce the down payment requirement on real estate loan even further.

Whatever you borrow from the mortgage lender as real estate loan needs to be paid back to the mortgage lender over a period of time (and, of course, you will also need to pay appropriate interest on that real estate loan).

The tenure of your real estate loan and the prevailing market rate will determine the amount of interest you pay for your real estate loan. Generally, you are required to pay back the real estate loan in the form of monthly instalments which are composed of both interest and principal portions of your real estate loan.

Also, there are various types of real estate loans e.g. fixed interest rate loans and adjustable interest rate loans. So depending on what type of real estate loan you have gone for, your monthly payments might either remain constant (fixed rate) for the full tenure of the loan or keep getting adjusted periodically (adjustable rate) on the basis of a financial index.

Besides that, some other costs are also associated with real estate loans e.g. there are closing costs, inspection costs, attorney fee etc.

Also, in case the property needs some repairs, there will be costs associated with that too. Again, there is stamp duty and other taxes that you need to pay. So really, you need to understand the concept of real estate loans and the related costs clearly before you actually go for the real estate loan. And understanding these concepts is really not that tough.

Getting the Best Mortgage Rate

Buying a home is an expensive endeavor so getting the best possible mortgage rate should be one of your main priorities. By deciding to get the best mortgage rate possible you will be making a positive decision to help you for many years to come.

However, just deciding to get the best mortgage rate available is not going to get you the best mortgage rate available. Instead, you will need to learn the tips and tricks for negotiating with your mortgage lender in order to receive the best possible mortgage rate for your personal situation.

Origination Fee

Your mortgage rate might be low in your mind, but you must take the origination fee into account as well because this can increase your APR. Lenders frequently charge 1%, but you can always negotiate the mortgage rate origination fee lower.

Also, if the origination fee is much higher than 1% you need to either negotiate it down, or find another lender with a more favorable overall mortgage rate.

Lock in the Rate

When negotiating your mortgage rate, make sure your lender is prepared to lock in your rate for at least 30-60 days. This way you will be guaranteed a particular rate even if rates skyrocket the next day.

Another not trick many individuals are not aware of is to include a clause that also will allow you to take a lower rate if rates fall during this period. This is a great mortgage rate tip because you get your mortgage rate locked in so it can't go any higher, but if the average mortgage rate goes lower you receive the lower rate.

Fight

If the mortgage rate drops significantly and you have already signed a deal locking in a particular mortgage rate and don't have a clause that ensures you will receive the lower rate, then you need to fight.

You simply need to call your lender and say that while you signed the lock in agreement you want the lower rate. This will take some negotiating, but your lender wants your business and might be willing to negotiate the mortgage rate with you.

Home FHA and Your Dream

For those people who are not familiar with the Federal Housing Administration (FHA), it is important to know that it is simply one of the branches of the government that has the basic function of being able to make sure that people can enjoy a better life, specifically through initiating a variety of housing programs for the citizens of the United States.

This is being done by the agency through insuring a big portion of the home loans that are being applied by many Americans today.

If you want to have your own house, one of the ways that can make such possible is to apply for a loan through the FHA. There are many people in the past who have decided to use this route, and it can be seen that they have been satisfied with such option.

If you plan on doing the same thing, there are some things that you should keep in mind.

One thing that you should understand is how the process works. Essentially, if you submit loan application through FHA, it is not the agency that provides for the loan. Rather, it just serves as the insurer of the loan that is applied to a mortgage broker.

If in case there are any problems associated with the payment of the person who has applied for the loan, the lender will have to go to FHA in order to solve the problem, and not directly to the borrower.

Because of this, there is a lower risk that is incurred by the lender, and there is a higher possibility that your mortgage loan will be approved, since it is backed up by a reliable government agency.

Aside from the higher possibility that you will be approved when a loan is applied through FHA, such is also beneficial because it can give you the opportunity to enjoy lower mortgage rates.

If you apply for a loan directly to a mortgage broker, the down payment that will be required can be as high as 15%. On the other hand, if you decide to apply for the same loan, the down payment that will be required through FHA can be as low as 3%. This will give you the opportunity to choose a better home.

Other ways at which it will be possible for you to save from a mortgage loan applied through FHA would be the fact they do not their lenders to charge high origination fees.

This fee is limited to less than 1%. More so, with the FHA, there is no more need to be charged with penalties for pre-payment. In the case of other mortgages, if you decide to hand in your payment in advance, you will be generally required to pay a certain percentage as part of the penalty for early payment.

If you are still looking for an affordable way to have you own home, and perhaps a way at which the likelihood of being approved is high, you should definitely consider approaching FHA.

Few Best Mortgage Deals for You

There are many times in life when we have to take a mortgage out. At times like this we often wonder what the best mortgage deal would be. It is a good idea to wait and watch for a good mortgage deal and not jump the gun.

This is because a house would be the single most expensive investment that we would make in our lives. Therefore it would be in our best interest to keep a good check on all the parameters that go into the deal.

Therefore a good research on the different types of mortgage deals will help us to get the best deal out of the lot.

When you look at the expenses of an average home owner, an miscalculated mortgage would mean that the person would end up paying a lot more than the cost of the house in mortgage.

This is why it is important that you make sure you know the type of the deal that you are getting into. After all, if you choose your plan carefully, you can make sure that you pay what you can every month and also the payments end when the price of your house is fully paid.

You can make an easy research over the type of mortgage on the internet. You can check out the rates for various mortgages and look for one that you think will fit you the best.

A mortgage can never be considered a glove to fit into any hand. If the situations are different, a particular type of mortgage can never be applied. This is because sine mortgages only will help in certain situations.

This is why there are different types of mortgages today. You should look through the different types of mortgages that are available. These different mortgages have their own unique features. Some of these might suite your needs and some of them don't.

Therefore you should look as to which deal fits your situation the best and go accordingly. This will make sure that your needs are well taken care of with the type of plan that you choose.

There are two types of mortgage deals generally. You can earthier choose the fixed rate mortgages or the adjustable rate mortgages. The fixed rate mortgages remain fixed with the inflation of the economy and you have to pay a constant rate of interest.

The adjustable interest rates change over time and with the economy. However, the range of the adjust-ability of the interest rate is dependent on the stipulations of the bank.

You have to therefore make sure that you know the range and also weather you will be able to pay the amount for interest for your mortgage. You should make sure that you know all the details of your mortgage before you enter into such a deal.

This will help you to make the right decisions and also to help you make a proper financial planning for your future that will help you purchase your dream house and also live in it.

Mortgage Insurance For Your Home

When buying a home, most of us will take out a mortgage to finance our new purchase. The provider of that mortgage, normally a bank or trust company, may require you take out a mortgage insurance policy to guarantee payment of the mortgage.

Should you die with a balance still owing, the bank, which owns the policy, will receive the balance of the payments in one lump sum. In this case, the survivors of the mortgage holder now own the house outright.

This is a group life insurance which you get by simply by ticking a box. However, the downside of this is that you are grouped together with people of varying ages and states of health; in other words, a typical group insurance policy.

If you are older and not in great health, this may be the way to go, though you should certainly confirm that you can't get a better rate.

It is very very easy just to agree and tick a box simply on the grounds that it takes no effort to do so. But that little tick can cost you hundreds of dollars more than you need to spend.

By far the majority of buyers should go to a broker who will look after their interests, not the interests of the bank. You need someone experienced to advise you on what you need and then to shop for that particular type of life insurance for you. You then have a list of companies and prices from which to make a choice.

You now have the mortgage insurance for the amount owing on your mortgage, and because you own it, not the bank, your survivors can decide what to do with the capital if you die. They could just continue the payments, pay off some of the capital owing or pay it off completely, their choice!

Doing it this way enables you to consider other reasons to take this mortgage insurance. Perhaps you also have a cottage or second home for which you also need mortgage insurance.

It is important to remember that "mortgage insurance" is term life insuranceArticle Submission, purchased for the purpose of paying off the mortgage. It is for this reason only that it is called mortgage insurance.

Chapter 9

The Huge Profits in Real Estate

Real estate is often termed as the safest investment avenue. In fact, real estate investments done with proper evaluation of the property (and its true value), can lead to good profits.

This is one reason why some people pursue real estate investment as their full time job. The talks of real estate are generally focussed towards residential real estate; commercial real estate seems to take a back seat. However, commercial real estate too is a good option for investing in real estate.

Commercial real estate includes a lot of different kinds of properties. Most people relate commercial real estate with only office complexes or factories/ industrial units. However, that is not all of commercial real estate.

There is more to commercial real estate. Health care centers, retail structures and warehouse are all good examples of commercial real estate. Even residential properties like apartments (or any property that consists of more than four residential units) are considered commercial real estate. In fact, such commercial real estate is much in demand.

So, is commercial real estate really profitable? Well, if it were not profitable I would not have been writing about commercial real estate at all. So, commercial real estate is profitable for sure.

The only thing with commercial real estate is that recognising the opportunity is a bit difficult as compared to residential real estate. But commercial real estate profits can be real big (in fact, much bigger than you would expect from residential real estate of the same proportion).

You could take up commercial real estate for either reselling after appreciation or for renting out to, say, retailers. The commercial real estate development is in fact treated as the first sign for growth of residential real estate. Once you know of the possibility of significant commercial growth in the region (either due to tax breaks or whatever), you should start evaluating the potential for appreciation in the prices of commercial real estate and then go for it quickly (as soon as you find a good deal).

And you must really work towards getting a good deal. If you find that commercial real estate, e.g. land, is available in big chunks which are too expensive for you to buy, you could look at forming a small investor group (with your friends) and buy it together (and split the profits later).

In some cases e.g. when a retail boom is expected in a region, you might find it profitable to buy a property that you can convert into a warehouse for the purpose of renting to small businesses.

So commercial real estate presents a whole plethora of investing opportunities, you just need to grab it.

Most Important Real Estate Investment Instruments

Real estate executors frequently require from me, what's the most fit promoting device real estate? Indeed, provided that I had a money for every time I caught this inquiry, I could be on an excursion at this very moment! So what are the best equipped showcasing instruments for real estate?

Well, I'm constantly speedy to express that you are your most fit real estate advertising instrument. Yes, you.The real estate executor perusing this piece. I've headed off so far as to compose a section concerning the most unbelievably compelling real estate advertising instrument, which is the executor outdated.

With the intention that programmable gets into the top-ten record of promoting apparatuses for real estate. Be that as it may what are the alternate nine? Here's my catalogue. Every day in your business region, hundreds (potentially many home purchasers and venders turn to the Web for real estate info.

Having a real estate web page is the first stride to joining with this best group of onlookers. What's the distinction among a network presence and a home page? Bounty. An online presence is a grain of sand on an extended shore, with small trust of standing out in any critical method.

Be that as it may a network presence builds the chance individuals will identify you within the web based world. A net presence combines such things as the real estate online content, within the web based world press discharges, real estate blogging and different within the web based world steps.

Your shots of bed. In an experience where such a variety of individuals utilize the online world of real estate explore, an unyielding net presence is an important showcasing device for real estate achievement.

In my assumption, real estate web journals might be one of the most unbelievably adequate showcasing instruments for real estate executors. Particularly when they're utilized legitimately.

When you distribute value matter to a real estate site on a normal premise, you are expanding your network presence. You're additionally positioning yourself as a power in your region. The proposed are simply a few of the explanations a Journal construct an exceptional promoting instrument for real estate achievement.

They can still be exceptionally effectual, specifically when mixed with some of the different showcasing channels on this page.

I regularly propose home-getting courses as a promoting device for real estate executors. No different real estate advertising method can transform a room full of potential clients, excited to catch what you need to express.

Granted, there are more than enough logistics included, but the prizes typically exceed the endeavour. Home getting workshops are most drastically adequate as a real estate showcasing instrument when directed in collaboration (i.e., A real estate executor teaming up with a home assessor, contract master, and whatnot.

It's no secret that client referrals head in a mess of business in the real estate industry. So in this respect, referrals are a weighty showcasing device for real estate executors.

Yet some executors neglect that the procedure hinting at an exceptional referral starts on Day 1 of the working association. Take great management of your customers from first contact to shutting day, and you'll tap into one of the most incredibly capable showcasing instruments for real estate, the client referral.

Chapter 10

Advances for Real Estate Agents

On account of real estate costs have dropped a significant spot, the potential requisitions that real estate operators and specialists might acquire have moreover dropped. Yet the drop in requisitions might be better than counterbalance by the product of real estates that might be sold.

And then getting value real estate heads is one of the keys to producing this an actuality for real estate masters. This is in light of the fact that there are such a variety of more real estates on the business sector now than there were when the air pocket blast.

The ascent in the number of homeowners who are underwater on their contracts has built so far that an exceptionally hefty number of them have chosen that they cannot manage to stay in their homes.

They could rather advertise their home and purchase a practically identical home for a much flatter cost, and take the misfortune with the intention that they are able to upgrade their money stream scenario by having a more level contract installment every month.

Then again a different outcome of the ascent in good to go real estates is that increasingly folks are coming to be first-time homeowners.

Seeing that costs on homes are falling, increasingly folks are equipped to bear a home for the same product they are at present paying in rent. So the legitimate decision for these individuals is to purchase a house as opposed to carrying on to rent.

The proposed elements all head to one thing-a higher require for real estate operators to assist the purchasing and offering of the sum total of the aforementioned real estates.

Subsequently, admitting that costs have fallen, the amount of good to go real estates, purchasers, and venders has raised which better than makes up for the more level costs in terms of what amount of a given real estate operator would be able to make in the present real estate business. Then again as we all know, the more customers a real estate executor has, the more real estates they'll push and the more cash they'll make.

Not just do they require more spearheads, they require fantastic spearheads provided that they are determined to be ahead of the game in changing over a heightened number of them into customers who in reality complete on getting or advertising one or more real estates.

One of the most effortless routes to get real estate heads is by obtaining them. There are ensembles whose sole reason is to identify folks who prefer to purchase or push a property. They then pitch this informative content to individuals who are ready to pay for it.

So assuming that you are a real estate operator searching for real estate spearheads and either don't have the chance to spot your particular, or basically would like to, then this would be a great choice for you.There are a few diverse major routes to do this.

You are able to buy the real estate spearheads from an ensemble as a set of information that you will get in the manifestation of a post or spreadsheet. Then you will begin filtering through them and utilizing the information good to go to qualify and sort them yourself.

Notwithstanding following that, the time is now to begin making exposes to spot they are valid spearheads or not.

How to Sell Real Estate via the Internet

Consumers have higher expectations than ever before in terms of a real estate site that offers valuable results where they can have all their needs met.

This makes it harder for modern estate agents to create the kind of site for real estate purposes that not only stand out from other sites, but exceeds customer expectations while helping the agent grow their real estate business.

What are some of the ingredients needed to help a real estate agent sell real estate via the internet?

Enhanced Listing Data to Improve Consumer Experience

Consumers in this day and age want to see a wide array of property listings on a real estate site, but that is not all. In addition, they would also like to interact with the property listing in one way or the other.

This would include the ability to simply click on a thumbnail to experience a larger, better view. They also want to take a virtual tour inside the advertised property. Modern technology made that consumers expect these things to be standard features of real estate sites.

Therefore, the modern agent need to stay competitive online and offer consumers what they want.

Luckily, there is a solution in that PG Real Estate Solution offer a wide array of options to help estate agents show off properties. This would include text description, video and image galleries, booking calendar, maps, and so on.

There are open source applications made available that can be installed on existing websites to enhance consumer experience. Not to mention the fantastic photo gallery programs where it is possible to upload several images in one sitting.

A really nice feature is that the estate agent can protect their listings through making use of watermarks or logos in order to prevent any list content stealing.

Using PG Real Estate will allow estate agents to showcase their listing on their own real estate site using panoramic style which will guarantee much more views than before.

Enhancing Website Usability

Real estate professionals will love the turnkey Multilingual Real Estate Script that allows them to manage site texts through the back-end which supports six languages such as English, Spanish, Russian, French, Turkish and German.

Visitors to real estate sites do not want to struggle to navigate their way around, and would certainly click away within mere seconds should they find that the site they are visiting makes is hard for them to find what they are looking for (Even on first visit).

The problem with real estate sites are that they fall short in many aspects. Most are cluttered with too many graphics and a lot of unnecessary information. In addition the menus are hard to find, and instructions on where to go is lacking.

Information is also poorly organized, making it difficult for consumers to find they way around the real estate site. These are all things that may reduce a real estate agent's chances of online success. Web users nowadays expect simplicity and organization.

This is why PG Real Estate Solution proves to be so popular with estate agents who want to be independent business owners with their own state of the art real estate site.

Chapter 11

Overview of Property Tax and Real Estate Exemptions

Property tax is assessed against residential and commercial real estate according to each state's tax assessment policies. Property taxes are used to pay for needs within county communities such as law enforcement and firefighter salaries, improvements to existing schools, building of new schools, and road and infrastructure repairs.

Property tax is calculated by multiplying the assessed property value times the state tax rate. For example, if the state tax rate is 5-percent and appraised property value is $100,000, the annual tax rate would be $5,000.

Property taxes are paid on an annual basis, but most states allow homeowners to pay in two installments. Using the calculation above, property owners would pay $2500 per installment. Homeowners would need to set aside $416.66 per month to cover their tax bill. This amount is in addition to their monthly home loan payment.

Mortgage lenders often include estimated taxes in the mortgage loan and funds are placed in an escrow account. Lenders hold escrowed funds until tax installments are due and submit payments to the county tax collector on behalf of homeowners. If banks do not withhold sufficient funds, homeowners are responsible for any deficiency amount.

If mortgage providers do not include property taxes in the home loan borrowers must pay taxes directly to their tax collection office. When homeowners fail to pay assessed property tax, mortgage providers may consider the loan to be in default and can initiate foreclosure proceedings. The real estate can be sold to pay tax debts.

Property tax bills are usually divided into three categories including: school districts, county and municipality. Approximately 60- to 70-percent of property taxes are allocated to schools to cover education costs. The remaining 30- to 40-percent are distributed amongst county and local government agencies.

Tax rates remain unchanged unless increases are passed through government legislation. Property tax assessments are subjective and often vary from year to year. Multiple factors are involved when assessing real estate values.

Real estate appraisers can assess property values on comparative sales reports of other properties in the area which have sold within the previous six months. Other factors may include the historical value of the real estate or potential value if the property is used to generate income through house flipping, rental, lease-to-own, or seller carry back trust deeds.

Property owners have the right to contest tax assessment if they feel they are being overcharged. Government agencies and tax assessors do make mistakes, so it is important for homeowners to check each valuation statement for accuracy. Things to look for include: correct address, lot size, number of rooms, and square footage.

Contesting tax assessments requires time and patience. In most cases, homeowners must schedule an appointment with a property tax representative. Homeowners should always retain previous years' tax bills in order to compare previously reported information. If mistakes are discovered, adjustments are reflected in future tax bills as opposed to providing refund checks.

Property owners should take time to determine if they qualify for any tax exemptions. The most common is the Homestead exemption which allows taxpayers to deduct exemptions for real estate used as a primary residence.

Homestead exemptions are usually a fixed amount. Florida provides a $25,000 exemption, while Louisiana exempts the first $75,000 and California exempts the first $7,000. As you can see, homestead exemptions can vary greatly by state.

Mortgage lenders can provide estimated property taxes and exemptions when borrowers obtain a new home loan or enter into mortgage refinancing. Prior to filing annual tax returns, property owners should consult with a qualified tax accountant to ensure they receive all available tax deductions.

The Differences Between Property Taxes and Real Estates Taxes

If you are new to the world of real estate, you might be a bit confused by all of the taxes that get assessed. To many people, the words 'property taxes' and 'real estate taxes' sound like they are the same, but there are some significant differences. Let's take a look at them.

Real estate taxes are taxes based on the property's assessed value. They are assessed on privately owned properties and funds are collected by local governments. Real estate taxes are the ones we often hear about that fund schools and pay for road repairs.

Property taxes have two sub-categories. There are certainly real property taxes that are real estate taxes, but there are also personal property taxes. Think of real property as something that cannot be moved. These are things like the house, an external garage, a storage building, or a barn.

Personal property is defined as things that can be moved, like furniture. These taxes are sometimes called excise taxes. Your car is also personal property. Believe it or not, but that licensing fee you pay for your car is a type of personal property tax.

If you have a business that repairs items or sells merchandise, that inventory is personal property. In many cases, you are exempt from taxes on the first

$50,000 or $100,000 of inventory, depending on your state.

If you own an RV, this is counted as personal property because it can be moved, even though you might be living in one full time. If it is sitting on land you own, you might have to pay real estate taxes on that land, but not in combination with the RV.

So what is the assessed value that these taxes are based on? Each local government has a department that looks at what the value of a property really is. They look at the structure and the land value itself.

Sometimes they calculate these values separately and sometimes they are looked at together. The assessment rate is a lower percentage of the assessed value. For many areas, the assessment rate is 70% - 80%, which then reduces the value of the house, and therefore the amount that the tax rate is calculated against.

It should be noted that HOA or condo association fees are not the same as real estate or property taxes. Those fees go directly to the association to cover costs of common area repairs and maintenance.

Personal property taxes are assessed as a percentage of the value of the item. Each state and county will have their own regulations on how they calculate personal property taxes. Also, each state as well as the federal government allows for a tax deduction on personal income tax forms for real estate taxes that have been paid in a given year.

There are also exemptions that certain homeowners might qualify for that help reduce the tax burden.

These exemptions are often for wounded military, the disabled, and the elderly.

Hopefully this has helped clear up the differences between property taxes and real estate taxes. Though they sometimes do overlap, they are also quite different. It just depends on what the item is that is being taxed.

Chapter 12

The Work of a Real Estate Broker

Buyers, particularly first-time buyers, find the help of real estate agents to be quite ideal when they are looking for homes for sale or they are collecting information on recent sales as well as the neighborhoods.

A real estate broker will help you identify long term value in the property that you want to purchase, and he or she will also help you negotiate the prices and make sure that the deal goes through successfully.

In simpler terms, what the real estate broker does is to find homes to sell as well as for buyers to buy them.

The real estate brokers usually help homeowners sell their home and also buyers to get the homes they want by making phone calls or they could also get referrals from other offices and also friends and family.

In some states, for one to become a real estate broker, they have to be licensed. They should be more educated compared to realtors. If you are a realtor and you want to become a broker, it usually takes you about another year of education.

This is because you will need to know all details about your marketing area, mortgage loans, and financial institutions in the area, veteran loans, VA loans as well as other programs.

The real estate broker is also in charge of overseeing sales associates as well as their listings. He or she needs to have a trust account. He or she is the one who is in charge of paying the bills and also taking care of advertising.

In the event of a dispute among the associates, he or she is the one who settles it. The broker's main concern is usually the legal aspect. He or she is legally responsible for all the things that take place in the office. And for such reasons, he or she will likely carry insurance.

The real estate broker holds office meetings and also works with his or her associates to make sure that they set meaningful goals and work towards them. He or she should be available to offer help, advice and guidance whenever it is needed.

When recruitment needs to be done in order to find new sales associates, he or she is the one who will be in charge of it. In order to make more sales, the real estate broker needs to have more agents in his office.

Another task that the real estate broker is entitled to is doing listings as well as selling of the properties. It is the broker who deals with most of the sales of most businesses or commercial properties.

He or she is also in charge of helping negotiate sales contracts. Other tasks he or she entitled to include handling leases of the homes, rental properties as well as apartments and businesses. It is also his or her mandate to manage these properties. He or should would collect earnest money and also prepare and sign contracts.

What is Real Estate Call Capture?

Most real estate professionals offer a toll free number on "for sale" signs and other marketing pieces. Today many of those phone numbers are answered by an automated system, which delivers information to callers 24 hours a day, generating real estate leads whether the office is open or not.

The technology behind the 24 hour information line is called "call capture."

These innovative systems allow real estate agents to assign different extension numbers to different ads or properties and then provide valuable information to prospective clients within those extensions.

By providing this information, agents are able to generate quality, real time leads for buyers and sellers. Most systems also allow for ad tracking so that agents can track where the most real estate leads are coming from.

Call capture is win-win for both the agent and the prospective customer. It is a sophisticated, yet simple to use, phone system where prospects can receive information anytime and anywhere it is convenient for them.

Consider a prospective home buyer driving around a desired neighborhood. The prospect sees a for sale sign in front of an interesting house. The sign gives a toll free number and offers to supply information about the property 24 hours a day.

The interested buyer places a quick call from the car and listens to a recording about some of the home's features. The prospect is pleased because he or she instantly obtains the desired information without waiting minutes or hours for a return call.

On the other end of the call, the call capture system records the phone number of the caller. Additional information, including the caller's name and address, can also be captured helping to generate real estate leads for an agent.

Addresses can be very valuable real estate leads to an agent as they can help in determining if the caller is a viable prospect; demographically, is the caller's neighborhood middle class or perhaps executive? Is the prospective buyer currently living in an apartment? Are they looking to upgrade or downgrade their housing?

Using the above example of a prospect calling from a cell phone while sitting outside of a listed property, think about what would happen without call capture.

The prospect might pick up a flyer, or try to call the real estate phone number listed on a for sale sign. If a call is made "after hours", then it either goes unanswered or is left in an office voice mail to be answered the next day when the prospect has only a vague recollection of the property.

The same scenario when using call capture is more dynamic. The prospect immediately has information on the property, so customer satisfaction is higher. The real estate professional has knowledge of who the prospect is and can quickly return the call, perhaps even while the prospect sits outside the property.

By calling into the hotline they have identified themselves and made themselves available as a prospective client.

Within minutes of a call (or even a hang up) to a call capture service or system, the agent can be notified via text, email message or voice mail. The call doesn't go "stale", giving the prospect time to call another property, and it gives the agent the power to respond how and when they choose.

As it identifies prospects, call capture also circumvents the "do not call" list. By law, calling those on the "do not call" list can result in hefty fines. However, if prospects call into a call capture system, then they have sought out information and fall under a 90 day inquiry period.

For 90 days the real estate professional can contact the prospect until the person tells them not to call back, opening up an entire pool of potential clients that would be otherwise inaccessible.

Many agents also use the call capture system to advertise free reports and other information that consumers are looking for. They can establish themselves as an expert in their area that consumers look to for quality information.

The real estate leads generation aspect of this kind of marketing is the same as with using the toll free number on a sign rider. When a caller dials in to get the free reports and information, the system will capture the lead and deliver it to the agent in real time.

Chapter 13

What a Real Estate Attorney Can Do for You

As you are searching for the house of your dreams, you may feel that the process will never end. And once you have found the house you want you need to realize that the process is not over. Now you have the negotiations for the final price of your home to work through.

Though many people choose to go through the negotiation process alone, you need to realize that it is not always as easy as it seems. Negotiations over the final contract price of a home can be lengthy and exhausting.

If you are a first time home buyer, it is even more important to realize that navigating the negotiation process can be difficult at best. That is why it may be in your best interest to hire an attorney that specializes in real estate to help you with your negotiation.

A real estate attorney will be able to help you with all the legal aspects of coming to a settlement with the seller.

It is important to realize that many times the cost of an attorney to help you with your real estate transaction can be pricey. But in the end the peace of mind that having an attorney on your side can be worth the expense.

Ask for referrals from your real estate agent before you hire a real estate attorney. Ensure that there is no conflict of interest between the attorneys you are considering and the property you are looking to purchase. This is very important to make sure you are getting the best representation.

Your friends and colleagues are good resources for you to use to find a referral as well. This can be an excellent way to find someone that you can trust. If you can't find someone through a referral you can also use the Internet to search for someone that will work for you.

Once you have narrowed down your list to a few possible lawyers, it is good to interview them in person or at least on the telephone. You can ask about their experience, their record and possibly references. This will give you the best idea if you will work well together.

Don't forget to get an idea of the charges that you will be billed for services provided. It is important to understand how you will be charged and when.

Keep your budget in mind when you are interviewing possible attorneys as well. With a little research you can get yourself good representation while purchasing your dream home.

Real Estate Litigations Require the Help of a Real Estate Attorney

As Houston is an important node in United States, the real estate industry has experienced a particular growth over the years. But whenever there is action, you have also conflicts and real estate industry is no exception.

In fact, real estate litigations have increased in numbers and diversity in the recent years. This is the point where you need a good and reliable Houston real estate lawyer.

Types of Real Estate Litigations

A Houston attorney specialized in real estate can provide a number of services which you are not qualified to handle or you don't have the time to do so. Litigation is a complex concept and real estate litigation is no different.

Real estate transactions are many times subject to dispute and the main reason is financial gain, loss, or compensation. Here is some information, outlining the actual aspects that a Houston real estate lawyer can deal with as far as real estate litigation goes.

- Fraud or non-disclosure defects conflicts which occur in various real property transactions

- Quiet title disputes which uses litigation to declare unsettled claims invalid

- Wrongful foreclosure by abusive lenders which may not have legal grounds for their action

- Conflicts with real estate agents or brokers who commit errors or abuse in certain circumstances

- Easement and neighbor disputes including conflicts over fencing, boundaries, and so other similar situations

- Zoning and land use disputes which are in most cases about wrongful law enforcement

- Enforcement of purchase agreements which must be initiated when one of the parties fails to complete the transaction

- Condemnation or eminent domain conflicts with the state wanting to turn private property into public domain

- Conflicts or disputes derived from the occurrence of Acts of God such as flooding, landslides, or subsidence

- Landlord-tenant disputes which are encountered more than often in the court of law

- Property damage disputes which need the assistance of a Houston real estate lawyer

- Private nuisance conflicts which are some of the oldest case laws in history

Estate litigation may occur between various entities depending on the type of transaction which led to the dispute. A good Houston real estate lawyer could prevent such litigations by supervising the transaction to start with. But in case a Houston attorney is not involved from the very beginning, litigation can occur.

Although sometimes it is too late, legal help is definitely required in most real estate litigations. If no argument will convince you to get a Houston real estate lawyer then remember what you stand to lose if you don't win your dispute.

In real property, the potential loss is huge just as the potential gain is. Therefore, all parties involved will struggle to have the best real estate Houston attorney representing their interests and winning their case. Real estate litigations are not to be left at the hands of luck. Action must be taken in order to reach your goals and the only solution is a real estate attorney.

The Many Tax Issue in Real Estate Law

Why is it important that you have knowledge about real estate law even as an ordinary buyer? There are lots of aspects in real estate that is controlled and regulated by real estate law.

The reason why should have have understanding about real estate law even when we are a regular buyer? Real estate law includes procedures and laws that wont only cover the buying and selling guide, but also cover the protection and the legal rights of the buyer when he made his investment.

Real estate is defined in the book as property that cannot be carried like land and all that is attached to it. In case you are serious to get a real estate, you should check these rules in order for you to stay clear of any problem.

What are the limitations placed?

There could be distinct regulations that are being implemented according to the state you're in as well as on the location of the property. One of such guidelines that you've is to check the state's zoning rules. Keep in mind any improvement undertaken on the building, such as size and height is ruled by guidelines.

It might be great to see whether the said property is free from dangerous radicals that could create a bad effect in the ecosystem like fuel, led paint, toxic waste products and compounds, and alike.

When it reaches to right of way, there is always a part in almost any property that may have to be made accessible when asked by the authorities for public access.

There are some limitations on property that the owner can demand, as trivial as the paint color to use on your property and house designs. As a future owner, you'll have to look at this so that you get full control over the property that you are about to invest in.

Property Lending, the Laws Behind It

When you are planning to buy a property which is to be borrowed by a lending institution, you will have to meticulously check the contract too. You may also discuss with a lawyer or attorney to review and clarify to you the entirety of the agreement for your own protection.

Tax Concerns

When you're the owner of a property, you will have to look into the matter of capital gains, specifically if the property you are selling is not your primary home.

The purchaser as well may need to give the transfer tax, however every thing still depends on the legal guidelines being enforced on the state where real property is located. You will also find some tax exemptions on property that your attorney can clarify to you.

In case you finally made a decision to buy the property, you will sign a deed of sale, before you sign, you have to make sure that the obligation of each party which happened to be you and the owner is indicated and offered on the contract in order for you to be sure you are covered as the new owner of the property in case any legal dispute pops up.

Relatively, when you buy property through a loan company, make sure that the contract you'll sign expresses your rights and commitments as the borrower and owner in addition to the rights and responsibilities of the lending institution.

Real estate law is there to generate a very good facilities on the system of purchasing and selling real estate properties giving out due protection for both the seller and the buyer. It is truly worth to check with a real estate law firm prior to getting into any transaction relative thereto.

Chapter 14

The Rise of Real Estate Infomercials

From the very beginning of the industry, real estate infomercials have been very successful. There's something about the idea of making money in real estate that appeals to a lot of people. In fact, most of the real estate infomercials that have appeared through the years have been scams for several reasons.

First the information that they purported to have, the secrets that only they knew but would sell to you for some small or not so small sum of money, were fairly common knowledge easily gleaned at a local library or available for free from the government.

Second, the "testimonials" from other, satisfied clients of the "plan" turned out to have been paid actors reading from a script and playing a role designed by the infomercial producers. And finally, some of them are using every advertising trick in the book to cover up the fact that they are outright lying.

The most famous example of real estate infomercials that turned out to be total frauds was a very successful program, that, to this day, many viewers remember seeing.

It stars a small, Vietnamese immigrant named Tom Vu who pitches his real estate magical formula from his mansion, his yacht or one of his many expensive cars while surrounded constantly with bikini clad swimsuit models.

What was Tom Vu selling? A seminar where he would reveal how he, a dirt poor immigrant, made a fortune in real estate and how you could copy his formula and get wealthy yourself by buying the information. What was he really selling?

Tom Vu sold the bodies of those gorgeous swimsuit models. Most people sat transfixed, watching this opulent display of wealth and flesh, hearing very little of what was actually being said and instantly got hooked.

Before they knew it they were calling and signing up for old Tom's seminar not because they were so taken with him and what he was saying, but because somehow he made them believe that they could be surrounded with beautiful women, just like Tom. If that little, funny looking guy could do it, then so can I!

Somehow, this worked. Tom has had some legal problems over this venture and the only secret he had to sell was the secret of making infomercials that mesmerized an audience into calling and spending some money without ever really knowing why.

This was early on in the growth of the industry when there was little accountability, but even so, Tom Vu was the model for almost all of the real estate infomercials that followed through the years.

Nowadays, real estate infomercials have learned how to use some of the fantastically successful Tom Vu techniques and avoid the legal problems. They do deliver a product - a book, a guide, a history of profitable real estate transactions that could be followed and could be profitable.

You've all seen the young, good looking guy talking about the fortune he has made buying houses for no money down, fixing them up and then selling them for a profit. Have you noticed he's sitting poolside in Hawaii talking with one of his clients, a beautiful woman in a skimpy bathing suit?

Tom Vu technique. Or the guy telling you how he's bought nothing but foreclosures and turned them over quickly for a healthy profit? He'll sell you a detailed guide of how he does what he does and a list of where to find foreclosures that you can get for free from the government just by making a few toll free phone calls. Is it worth it? You decide.

Managing Your Real Estate Property

Now that you have started your real estate venture and you're working with a property or two, there are a few things that you will need to learn when it comes to making sure that you're business runs smoothly. If you have a string of properties, it may be a good idea to decide if you'd be better off utilizing a property manager to take care of things for you.

Owning so many properties at once can get very hectic because of the maintenance and upkeep, so if you don't have the time to maintain them, it's best to have someone help you so that your business won't suffer.

Finding a suitable tenant!

After you have fixed up your property and it is now in livable condition, the first thing you must do is select a tenant. This is the single most important part of your business. The most vital factor in the type of tenant you will attract is the area in which you have chosen to buy property.

It is important that you screen your applicants, carefully and seriously. You could run into a multitude of problems if you aren't thorough in your selection of a tenant.

You'll want to come up with rental criteria, a list of things that your potential tenant will need to provide you with, so that you can carefully evaluate if they are a good match for you and your property that you've worked so hard to not only attain but also maintain.

Good help is hard to find!

Another task in managing your properties is finding quality Tradesmen/Craftsmen. This is almost as important as finding a tenant and the process is similar. In finding quality workers, it's a good idea to set up criteria and what you are looking for.

This person will be responsible for doing the maintenance repairs for your rental properties, so you want to ensure that they are qualified to perform the duties that you will most certainly need done when it's time to fix your properties.

Talk with friends, people that you know very well and can take their word when it comes to referring a professional to you. Also, if you have seen their work with your own eyes, that's another plus. This means that you can attest to the fact that this person will do a great job for you.

Once you have found a pool of candidates to interview for your job, some questions that you might want to ask are, if they have previously done the specific type of work that you are requesting and how long will the specific job take.

Once you have found the right person for the job and they have completed the task, it's a good idea to check over their work just to make sure that the job was done to your satisfaction.

Accurate Accounting

Owing property of course means keeping accurate accounting records. It is best practice to have an automated system that will handle all of your financial records for you. There are a number of programs available such as, Quick Books.

This software will allow you to keep track of all your financial transactions and help you balance each month. There are other types of property management software available that can help you stay on track.

It is up to you what system you'd like to use but make sure you have something in place. You want to keep the paperwork intact and the money rolling in. Good record keeping makes filing your tax returns easy!

Chapter 15

"The Royal Flush" of Investing in Real Estate

There are many options for investing your money. Here are some examples:

- o Stocks
- o Bonds
- o Bank Certificates
- o Mutual Funds
- o Other Over the Counter Investments
- o REAL ESTATE

Department store tycoon Marshall Field once said "Real estate is not only the best and quickest way to make you wealthy, for the average person it is truly the only way."

What makes real estate such a great investment for the average person? Why have so many wealthy people used real estate to amass their fortunes? The answer is- Only with real estate do you get "The Royal Flush".

What does a royal flush have to do with real estate? Here is what I mean. Every kind of investment has some advantages and the more advantages the better the investment. For example with IRA's there are tax advantages and with stocks you may have leverage through a margin account.

Real estate on the other hand has five advantages and all five cannot be found in any other investment. I call these "The Royal Flush" because having all of them makes it hard to lose.

Only with real estate do you have the advantages of :

- o Leverage
- o Inflation
- o Revenue Production
- o Tax Advantages
- o The Power of Compound Interest

Let's look at each of these separately:

Leverage - The Geek Inventor and Mathematician Archimedes once said "Give me a lever long enough and a fulcrum on which to place it and I shall move the world." Leverage will allow you to control a $100,000.00 property for a little as $10,000.00 possibly even less.

When you mix this leverage with just a 3% Inflation your $10,000.00 investment just grew by 30% and that kind of return is very difficult to find with any other investment.

Inflation - Median Housing Costs in the U.S. in 1940's was $2,000.00. By the 1970's it had jumped to $23,000.00 and by 2007 it was over $150,000.00. Don't be misled by news reports that insist that the real estate bubble is going to burst.

People will always need a place to live and real estate will always hold value. History clearly shows that real estate always has been and always will be a good investment.

Revenue Production - Wouldn't it be nice if you could borrow $10,000.00 - put it into the stock market and then take that stock and rent it out to so that that rent would more than cover your loan payments. That may sound ridiculous--but it's done every day with real estate.

Tax Advantages - Democratic Governments love real estate investors and give them tax advantages to prove it. Even thought home prices may go up in a given year in most cases the owners are allowed to take a tax deduction for the depreciation of that same home. There are also deductions for repairs, taxes paid, interest, and the list goes on and on.

The Power of Compound Interest - Albert Einstein called Compound Interest "The 8th Wonder of the World." Has anyone ever ask you if you would rather have a thousand dollars a day for a month or a penny a day doubled for a month.

The thousand a day would net you $31,000 in January but the penny a day doubled each day would net you $5,368,708.80. That's just one example of the power of compound interest. By reinvesting the profits from your investments you will receive similar results in just a few short years.

Using your Royal Flush it will only take one home per year to create wealth.

"Over the years"

§ Rents will go up
§ Principal pay down will increase
§ Property value should appreciate
§ Tax advantages will add up
§ Mortgages will eventually payoff

And you become wealthy.

Chapter 16

What is Real Estate Text Marketing?

It seems that the whole world has gone text crazy. Walk down the street in any town and you will see people of all ages tap-tap-tapping on their cell phones. So as a real estate agent you may say to yourself, "Okay, sure but what does that have to do with me?"

Well it has plenty to do with you. Texting has become one of the most popular, efficient and preferred methods of communication. Recognizing this, companies have developed technology that allows real estate agents to provide information on listings and other services that they offer in a way that people want to get it - through text message.

Real estate text marketing allows an agent to attach a sign rider to their property sign that includes a toll free phone number and unique code for each property.

When an interested buyer drives by the home they are able to dial the toll free number from their cell phone and receive a text message back with information about the property - photos, description, virtual tour, video.

The agent is then notified of the call on the property and can follow up with the potential buyer.

In this way, it works much like a more traditional 800 call capture system in that it generates leads for the agent. The major difference being in the way the information is being delivered to the caller.

While real estate text marketing technology is still relatively new, those agents that are on the leading edge and have already incorporated text marketing into their advertising campaigns, are telling of some major benefits.

The ability to generate and capture leads 24/7. It doesn't matter what time day or night the potential buyer is looking at the property, they are able to get a text message that will give them the information they are looking for and can further interest them in the home.

Save money. No more brochures to print. Agents are saving up to 50% using text marketing versus print brochures.

Get more listings. Real estate agents demonstrating their text marketing campaign at listing presentations are getting more sellers. Home sellers are impressed with the technology and can see how it will help them sell their home.

Real estate text marketing agents is measureable. Agents are able to run reports of leads generated and see how well buyers are responding to the campaign.

It is easy to use - especially a real estate text marketing service that allows users to call into a toll free number versus having to text a code in order to receive the property information. The process is easy enough that people of all ages and levels of cell phone experience will be able to use it.

A quality real estate text marketing service will be able to deliver property information in multiple languages as well. Agents are finding they are now able to reach multiple demographics for their properties.

Go green. Agents are reducing their carbon footprint by using this technology. They no longer need to print brochures or use up the additional resources it takes to drive around and replenish the brochures when all the neighbors come by and take them.

Understanding a new technology is the first step in knowing whether or not it will fit in with your real estate business. Such is the case with text marketing. It is a powerful way to generate and capture leads while communicating the information consumers are looking for, in the way that they prefer to receive it.

Conclusion

Real estate investing can be very intimidating and it's easy for a new investor to be paralyzed with fear even in the presence of the "deal of a lifetime." The truth is that real estate investing is a number analysis game that can easily be stopped by emotions.

To keep yourself from getting overwhelmed and hiding under a rock, be aware of your motivation for investing. Are you looking to eliminate debt? Are you looking to secure a financial future? The vision of your purpose will keep you in the game.

There are many, many, many ways to make money in real estate. So, to avoid being swayed by the "deal frenzy," you should always select your investing strategy based on what you already decided that you wanted financially.

This will keep you from buying cheap vacant land when what you really want is cash flow. No matter how tempting that cheap vacant land is, it's not in line with your goals. Pass it up or change your goals.

Once people find out that you're a real estate investor, deals will start coming out of the woodworks and you will be tempted every day by the "deal of a lifetime." What do you do? Consult your investing rules and decide if the deal is in harmony or in conflict with those rules.

Knowing what you want, what your investing strategy is and what resources you have available are will help you set parameters and guidelines for investing. And that in turn, will keep your risk of losing money down as low as possible.

It's easy to be seduced by the profit potentials of Real estate investing. That's why you need to make your investing decisions up front without the deal in front of you to distract you.

The biggest mistake that new investors make is to buy properties on a whim without a plan. They spend more time trying to get out of their bad deal and less time making more money.

Learn to keep your risk down and get educated on real estate investing. Learn to create a realistic investing plan to keep your profits high and the risk of losing money with real estate investing as low as possible.

With this exposure on investing in real estate, guess you are ready to plunge into the business, but watch your back for bad guys disguising as agents.

From the author's desk: Reviews are gold to authors. If you've enjoyed this book, would you consider rating it and reviewing it on Amazon.com?

Thank you in anticipation and wishing you all the best in the world of real estate investment.